BEI GRIN MACHT SICH IHR WISSEN BEZAHLT

- Wir veröffentlichen Ihre Hausarbeit,
  Bachelor- und Masterarbeit

- Ihr eigenes eBook und Buch -
  weltweit in allen wichtigen Shops

- Verdienen Sie an jedem Verkauf

Jetzt bei www.GRIN.com hochladen und kostenlos publizieren

Philipp Kock

The Depiction of Violence and the Soldier's everyday life in Michael Herr's "Dispatches" and Tim O'Brien's "The Things they carried"

GRIN Verlag

Bibliografische Information der Deutschen Nationalbibliothek:

Die Deutsche Bibliothek verzeichnet diese Publikation in der Deutschen National-
bibliografie; detaillierte bibliografische Daten sind im Internet über http://dnb.d-
nb.de/ abrufbar.

Impressum:

Copyright © 2008 GRIN Verlag GmbH
Druck und Bindung: Books on Demand GmbH, Norderstedt Germany
ISBN: 978-3-640-73101-5

Dieses Buch bei GRIN:

http://www.grin.com/de/e-book/159636/the-depiction-of-violence-and-the-soldier-
s-everyday-life-in-michael-herr-s

The Depiction of Violence and the
Soldiers' everyday life in
Michael Herr's *Dispatches* and
Tim O'Brien's *The Things they carried*

Table of Contents

1. Introduction

1.1 Topic statement

Michael Herr's *Dispatches* and Tim O'Brien's *The Things they carried* (I will use the abbreviation *Things*) are two well-known examples of Vietnam War Literature. *Things* approaches the Vietnam War as "a work of fiction". The author states in the beginning of his book: "Except for a few details regarding the author's own life, all the incidents, names and characters are imaginary". Critics refer *Things* to Postmodernism.

Dispatches, however, is not fiction: Michael Herr covered the war for 2 years (1967-69) for the Esquire magazine and in 1978, the year of the publication, *Dispatches* was nominated for the National Book Award for nonfiction (Bonn 28). The critics label Dispatches as New Journalism:

> "Michael Herr's Dispatches is the work of a war correspondent, but it is not journalism in the ordinary sense of the word, i.e. an objective, detached reporting of the "facts". Instead it is a work of the so-called New Journalism, a hybrid form that, in typical postmodern fashion, blurs traditional genre distinctions. (...) The New Journalism abandons all pretense of impersonal objectivity instead an intense, substituting subjectivity that (...) also employs such devices of fiction as characterization, flashbacks and interior monologue" (Carpenter 36/37).

This term paper deals with the depiction of the Vietnam War in *Dispatches* and *Things*, with a special focus on the depiction of violence and the everyday life of the soldiers. Because of the fact that the books are different in style and narrative transmission, I will put briefly some emphasis on those aspects in the beginning.

1.2 Thesis statement

Both writers depict the war without moral purposes, showing as well the negative features of the war (death, terror, fear, brutalization, deadening, etc.) as the properties of war which could be regarded as "positive" (a thrilling and seductive experience, comradeship, "beauty"/"majesty" of the war).

2. Main Part

2.1. Style and Narrative transmission in *Dispatches* and *The Things they carried*

First of all, I want to compare the physical setup of *Dispatches* and *The Things they carried*. *Dispatches* is written as one single Vietnam War report by the Esquire correspondent Michael Herr, consisting of several vignettes. *Things* is composed of twenty-two stories that can be read independently but "the intent is clearly that this text be read not just as a collection of independent stories but also as a unit" (Tegmark 204). Herr employs all the time the same narrator, namely the autodiegetic, first-person narrator "Michael Herr the Vietnam War correspondent", who tells what he has seen with his own eyes and what soldiers, correspondants and other persons have told him:

> "I remembered the way a Phantom pilot had talked about how beautiful the surface-to-air missiles looked as they drifted up towards his plane to kill him, and remembered myself how lovely .50-calibre tracers could be, coming at you as you flew at night in a helicopter, how slow and graceful, arching up easily, a dream, so remote from anything that could harm you" (Herr 132).

O'Brien, however, uses different techniques of narrative transmission: There are two different "Tim O'Briens", first "Tim O'Brien the middle-aged veteran" (Tegmark 205) and "Tim O'Brien the young soldier"(Tegmark 204). Additional, there also some "secondary narrators, (...) they tell a story which "Tim O'Brien, the middle-aged veteran, then passes out to his narratee" (Tegmark 204/205). Lieutenant Jimmy Cross is one example for such a secondary narrator who substitutes O'Brien as a narrator. He presents the first of the two narrative lines in the opening title story "The Things they carried", telling the story of Cross' Love for Martha and his feeling of fuilt for the death of Ted Lavender (Tegmark 245/246). The other narrative line is done by a "very overt and seemingly omniscient narrator" (246) who tells the perspective of the "average grunt" (246).

The middle-aged veteran narrator "refers to himself as "Tim O'Brien", the author of the very narrative he is narrating, thus giving the impression of autobiography" (Tegmark 206). In *In the Shoes of a Soldier* Mats Tegmark compares this narrator with the narrator of *If I die in a Combat Zone* and he comes to the conclusion that the narrator of *Things* is "much more overt" than *If I die in a Combat Zone* (Tegmark 206). I agree that the narrator is overt because the requirement, that for an overt narrator "the narrator appears on the level of narrative transmission as an individualized speaker or concrete persona" is given: "Many years after the war Jimmy Cross came to visit me at my home in Massachusetts, and for a full day we drank coffee and smoked cigarettes and talked about everything we had seen and done so long ago, all the things we still carried through our lives" (O'Brien 25). Another proof for the overtness of this narrator is that "the middle-aged writer and veteran "Tim O'Brien", the author of these very stories; as such he not only comments on the stories he is telling in this volume, but also refers to other O'Brien books, in a kind of intertextual and metafictional gesture":

> "As the novel developed over the next year, and as my own ideas clarified, it became apparent that the chapter had no proper home in the larger narrative. Going after Cacciato was a war story; Speaking of Courage was a postwar story. Two different time periods, two different sets of issues. There was no choice but to remove the chapter entirely. The mistake, in part, had been in trying to wedge the piece into a novel" (O'Brien 158).

A final important evidence for the overtness of this narrator is that he also employs some excursus of "how to tell a true war story: A true war story is never moral. It does not instruct, nor encourage virtue, nor suggest models of proper human behaviour, nor restrain men from doing the things men have always done. If a story seems moral, do not believe it." (O'Brien 68). Tegmark labels this narrator as "highly unreliable" (Tegmark 206) because O'Brien writes:

> "I want you to feel what I felt. I want you to know why story-truth is truer sometimes than happening truth. Here is the happening-truth. I was once a soldier. There were many bodies, real bodies with real faces, but I was young then and I was afraid to look. (...) Here is the story-truth. He was a slim, dead, almost dainty young man of about twenty. He lay in the center of a red clay trail near the village of My Khe. His jaw was in his throat. His one eye was shut, the other eye was a star-shaped hole. I killed him" (O'Brien 179).

2.2. Commonalities in depicting the Vietnam War in *Dispatches* and *Things*

By dealing with the depiction of war in both books it is not possible to separate the scrutinized aspects violence and the everyday life of the soldiers because these two aspects are entangled with each other: Violence and Death belong to the everyday life of the combatants.

This permanent confrontation with violence and death results in a brutalization of the soldiers, which becomes obvious in *Dispatches* and *Things*: "There was a famous story, some reporters asked a door-gunner, 'How can you shoot women and children?' and he'd answered, 'It's easy, you just don't lead 'em so much'" (Herr 34). In *Things* the death of an American soldier is retaliated by destroying the Vietnamese village of Than Khe: "They burned everything. They shot chickens and dogs, they trashed the village well, they called in artillery and watched the wreckage (…)"(O'Brien 14).

Another brutal scene of revenge takes place when the platoon comes across a "baby VC water buffalo":

> "He stepped back and shot it through the right front knee. The animal did not make a sound. It went down hard, then got up again, and Rat took careful aim and shot off an ear. He shot it in the hindquarters and in the little hump at its back. (…) It wasn't to kill; it was to hurt. (…) Nobody said much. The whole platoon stood there watching, felling all kind of things, but there wasn't a great deal of pity for the baby water buffalo" (O'Brien 75).

Death becomes so omnipresent that the soldiers lose piety:

"The living, the wounded and the dead flew together in crowded Chinooks, and it was nothing for guys to walk on top of the half-covered corpses packed in the aisles to get a seat, or to make jokes among themselves about how funny they all looked, the dumb dead fuckers" (Herr 24). Another examples for the loss of respect towards dead comrades are when Curt Lemon is killed by a rigged artillery round and his extremities are blown onto a tree: "The gore was horrible, and stays with me. But what wakes me up twenty years later is Dave Jensen singing 'Lemon Tree' as we threw down the parts" (O'Brien 78/79) and a scene from Dispatches: "The old hostility of the grunt towards Marine Air became total on 861: when the worst of it was over and the first Ch-34 finally showed over the hilltop, the door gunner was hit by enemy ground fire and fell out of the chopper.

It was a drop of over 200 feet, and there were Marines on the ground who cheered when he hit" (Herr 123). The general deadening of the soldiers leads to atrocious deeds, for example, Mitchell Sanders cuts of the thumb of a dead Vietcong and gives it to Norman Bowker as a good-luck charm (O'Brien 11/12) and the young Mary-Anne who got seduced by the war wears a necklace of human tongues (O'Brien 103). And there is also the story "about the kid who had mailed a gook ear home to his girl and could not understand now why she had stopped writing to him" (Herr 148).

The soldiers are aware of the fact that death lurks everywhere:

> "You could die in a sudden bloodburning crunch as your chopper hit the ground like dead weight, you could fly apart so that your pieces would never be gathered, you could take one

neat round in the lung and go out hearing only the bubble of the last few breaths, you could die in the last stage of malaria with that faint tapping in your ears, and that could happen to you after months of firefights and rockets and machine guns. (...) You could end in a pit somewhere with a spike through you, everything stopped for ever except for the one or two motions, purely involuntary, as though you could kick it all away and come back. You could fall down dead so that the medics would have to spent half an hour looking for the hole that killed you, getting more and more spooked as the search went on. You could be shot, mined, grenaded, rocketed, mortared, sniped at, blown up and away so that your leavings had to be dropped into a sagging poncho and carried to Graves Registration, that's all she wrote. It was almost marvellous" (Herr 133/134).

The soldiers try to cope with the constant threat of death by using "a hard vocabulary to contain the terrible softness" (O'Brien 17). Lucas Carpenter states that "O'Brien is (...) aware of the "sliding signifiers" that words become when applied to the war" (Carpenter 48): "I learned that words make a difference. It's easier to cope with a kicked bucket than a corpse; if it isn't human, it doesn't matter much if it's dead. And so a VC nurse, fried by napalm, was a crispy critter. A Vietnamese baby which lay nearby, was a roasted peanut. "Just a crunchie munchie," Rat Kiley said as he stepped over the body" (O'Brien 231). The American soldiers have their own language, they talk "grunt lingo" (O'Brien 17).

As Bennett puts it,

"Within O'Brien's own manipulation of language (...) in The Things they carried lies what may have been his deeper linguistic inspiration: the lexicon of the front line. The mouths of the men of Alpha Company brim with a wide array of euphemisms and double-speak designed by the troops, consciously or not, to distance themselves from the trauma of war" (Bennett 66).

Death is so everyday for the soldiers that it is almost routine to them. This becomes also obvious in the scenes in which the Graves Registration (the agency in the US forces which is responsible for gathering the corpses of the fallen American soldiers for sending them home) occurs: "They stripped off Lavender's canteens and ammo, all the heavy things, and Rat Kiley said the obvious, the guy's dead, and Mitchell Sanders used his radio to report one US KIA and to request a chopper. (...) They carried him out to a dry paddy, established security, and sat smoking the dead man's dope until the chopper came" (O'Brien 7). In Dispatches this routine becomes even more illuminated: "'If you get hit,`a medic told me, 'we can chopper you back to base-camp hospital in like twenty minutes.` 'If you get hit real bad,` a corpsman said, 'they'll get your case to Japan in twelve hours.` If you get killed,`a spec 4 from Graves promised, 'we'll have you home in a week`'" (Herr 21).

But besides the constant fear of being killed, the soldiers suffer also from the other extreme, boredom:

> "If you weren't humping, you were waiting. I remember the monotony. Digging foxholes. Slapping mosquitos. (...) Even in the deep bush, where you could die any number of ways, the war was nakedly and aggressively boring. (...) It was boredom with a twist, the kind of boredom that caused stomach disorders. (...) You'd try to relax. You'd uncurl your fists and let your thoughts go. Well, you'd think this isn't so bad. And right then you'd hear gunfire behind you and your nuts would fly up into your throat and you'd be squealing pig squeals. That kind of boredom" (O'Brien 33).

To deal with both extremes, death and boredom, the soldiers and correspondants consume drugs and alcohol: "In the Highlands (...) I got stoned with some infantry from the 4ᵗʰ. One of them had worked for months on his pipe, beautifully carved and painted with flowers and peace symbols" (Herr 33) and "(...) I also have a bottle. ('Oh man, you're welcome here. Your are *definitely* welcome. (...)" (Herr 110). In *Things* the men of Alpha Company "sat smoking the dead man's dope" (O'Brien 7) when Ted Lavender got killed. Lavender himself, used to calm himself down by tranquillizers: "'How's the war today?' somebody would say, and Ted Lavender would give a soft, spacey smile and say, 'Mellow, man. We got ourselves a nice mellow war today'" (O'Brien 32).

Another burden that the soldiers have to bear is the hostile nature of vietnam, the climate is hot and moist, the men suffer from jungle diseases and parasites and the thick vegetation is the perfect hideout for the Vietcong: "They carried diseases, among them malaria and dysentery. They carried lice and ringworm and leeches and paddy algae and various rots and molds. They carried the land itself – Vietnam (...). They carried the sky. The whole atmosphere, they carried it, the humidity, the monsoons, the stink of fungus and decay, all of it (...)" (O'Brien 12/13) and "There were times when your fear would take direction so wild that you had to stop and watch the spin. Forget the Cong, the trees would kill you, the elephant grass grew up homicidal, the ground you were walking over possessed malignant intelligence, your whole environment was a bath" (Herr 62).

But despite of all the violence and terror, many soldiers are not able to disengage themselves from the war. For example, a young soldier who is allowed to leave the besieged US base Khe Sanh, misses each time his transport-helicopter on purpose:

> "The next morning two of his friends went with him to the edge of the strip and saw him into the trench. ('Goodbye,'Gunny said. 'And that's an order.') They came back to say he'd gotten out for sure this time. An hour later he came up the road again, smiling. He was still there the

first time I left Khe Sanh, and while he probably made it out eventually, you can't be sure" (Herr 91/92).

The "quick peace story" (O'Brien 33) describes the same phenomenon, a soldier falls in love with a Red Cross nurse, stays a while with her but

> "the nurse loves him to death – the guy gets whatever he wants whenever he wants it. The war's over, he thinks. (...) But then one day he rejoins his unit in the bush. Can't wait to get back into action. Finally one his buddies asks what happened with the nurse, why so hot for combat, and the guy says, 'All that peace, man, it felt so good it hurt. I want to hurt it back' (O'Brien 34).

Michael Herr and his correspondent colleagues cannot resist the temptations of war, too: "And every time, you were so weary afterwards, so empty of everything but being alive that you couldn't recall any of it, except to know that it was like something else you had felt once before. It remained obscure for a long time, but after enough times the memory took shape and substance and finally revealed itself one afternoon during the breaking off of a firefight. It was the feeling you'd had when you were much, much younger and undressing a girl for the first time" (Herr 135).

Another passage from *Dispatches* gives us a glimpse of how these temptations of war might look like: "Even the incoming was beautiful at night, beautiful and deeply dreadful. I remembered the way a Phantom pilot had talked about how beautiful the surface-to-air missiles looked as they drifted up towards his plane to kill him (...)" (132).

An even more clear example of the "positive things" of war is a passage near the end of Dispatches: Herr's correspondent friend Tim Page is asked by his publisher

> "to do a book whose working title would be 'Through with War'and whose purpose would be to once and for all 'take the glamour out of war', Page couldn't get over it. 'Take the glamour out of war ! I mean, how the bloody hell can you do that? Go and take the glamour out of a Huey, go take the glamour out of a Sheridan...Can you take the glamour out of a Cobra or getting stoned at China Beach? It's like taking the glamour out of a M-79 (...). Ohhhh war is good for you, you can't take the glamour out of that. It's like trying to take the glamour out of sex, trying to take the glamour out of the Rolling Stones.' 'Ohh, what a laugh! Take the glamour out of bloody war!" (Herr 248/49).

Bonn writes that Michael Herr "does not believe the glamour can be removed from war. It is a tough, bitter, bloody glamor, but glamor it remains nevertheless, and it is a glamour wich emanates from the hypermasculinity and sexually charged violence of war" (Bonn 38).

From these examples one can state that Michael Herr and Tim O'Brien depict war with the same themes and motives (see above), but how are Dispatches and Things comparable when scrutinizing the literary forms, Postmodernism and New Journalism?

2.3.   Depicting the war with Postmodernism and New Journalism

Many critics label the Vietnam War as a postmodern phenomenon because this war was a result of a political tumult in the US and Europe, which gave rise to postmodernism (Carpenter 32): "Indeed, the principal theoreticians of the postmodern -Lyotard, Foucault, Jameson, Deleuze, Baudrillard, and others- either participated in or were strongly affected by the turmoil of the 1960s, and their early expressions of postmodern theory appear in the shadow of the Vietnam War" (Carpenter 32). Carpenter states also, that this war also embodied many of the historical contingencies that fueled the rise of postmodernism: "First and foremost, it was largely a capitalist war fought to protect American political and economic interests in Southeast Asia by an American military organized and managed like a corporation working hand-in-glove with other American "businesses" (...)"(33). The term postmodernism refers "to certain radically experimental works of literature and art produced after World War II. Postmodernism is distinguished from modernism, which generally refers to the revolution in art and literature that occurred during the period 1910 through 1930, particularly following the disillusioning experience of World War I. The postmodern era, with its potential for mass destruction and its shocking history of genocide, has evoked a continuing disillusionment similar to that widely experienced during the Modern Period" (*The Bedford Glossary of Critical and Literary Terms*, 360).

A trademark of this era is that the postmodernists wanted to break away from traditions by experimentating with new literary devices, forms and styles (*Bedford Glossary*, 360). A result of these experiments is the New Journalism: "The ferment of social change of the last decades, and the exhaustion of certain forms of fiction that have dominated the novel since World War II, have created new opportunities for writers. One of the most interesting responses has been the creation of hybrid forms that combine fictional techniques with the detailed observation of journalism (...) Significantly, novelists have turned away from the necessity of inventing plots and characters to direct confrontations with social reality. The varieties of these works of fictionalized have been called a number of terms- "higher journalism", "new journalism", "the literature of fact" (Hollowell, 10).

Michael Herr could have employed conventional Journalism to cover the Vietnam War but he did not because he thinks: "Conventional Journalism could no more reveal this war than conventional firepower could win it, all it could do was take the most profound event of the American decade and turn it into a communications pudding, taking its most obvious, undeniable history and making it into a secret history" (Dispatches 220).

Bonn states that "Dispatches is fully engaged in the slippery relationship of fact, fiction, documentation and reportage and how these categories become infinitely entangled when applied to the historical, political, and experiential chaos of war" (Bonn 28). So Michael Herr does not claim to cover the Vietnam War in a objective way, instead he chooses "New Journalism (...) a form which arises out of the tensions between fact and fiction, objectivity and personal vision, bearing witness and bringing judgment" (Bonn 28).

Herr puts his vision of Vietnam into effect by using techniques that originate actually in the novel: "dramatic scenes, full dialogue, complex point of view, interior monologue (...)" (Bonn 30). But the most important feature in the way of dealing with the Vietnam War by New Journalism, is perhaps the language in which Dispatches is told:

> "He is also concerned (...) with innovation in language. Herr, with his transformation of conventional punctuation and sentence structure and jazzy, freely fluctuating rhythms performs linguistic alchemy, and by reordering syntax and punctuation and using a language which draws upon popular culture and contemporary discourses (...)" (Bonn 30).

A good example for Herr's special language might be:

> "Airmobility, dig it, you weren't going anywhere. It made you feel safe, it made you feel Omni, but it was only a stunt, technology. Mobility was just mobility (...), what you really needed was a flexibility far greater than anything the technology could provide, some generous, spontaneous gift for accepting surprises, and I didn't have it. I got to hate surprises, control freak at the crossroads, if you were one of those people who always thougt they had to know what was coming next, the war could cream you" (Herr 13).

Herr employs not only a pop culture (see above) language but also an authentic, rough language that was used by American soldiers in Vietnam, including swearwords as well as military abbreviations: "KIA Travel Bureau" for Graves Registration (22), "Lurp" for long-range recon patrollers, "zapped" for killed (25), "motherfuckers" (77), etc.

Tim O'Brien's language is rather similar to Herr's, he uses also a specific "grunt lingo"

11

(O'Brien 17) which has also popular culture- and contemporary- features and does not avoid swearwords, too: "Henry Dobbins asked what the moral was. Moral? You know. *Moral*. Sanders wrapped the thumb in toilet paper and handed it across to Norman Bowker. There was no blood. Smiling, he kicked the boy's head, watched the flies scatter, and said, It's like with that old TV show – Paladin. Have gun, will travel. Henry Dobbins thought about it. Yeah well, he finally said. I don't see no moral. There it *is*, man. Fuck off" (O'Brien 12).

This special language in both *Dispatches* and *Things* is typical for postmodernism because it is "non-traditional and against authority and signification" (Penguin Dictionary of Literary Terms & Literary Theory 690).

Dispatches features also a severe negative criticism of the general media, including also Hollywood: Herr writes that many American soldiers fall prey to the "John Wayne Wet dream"(Bonn 33), which means that they're behaving careless in perilous combats when they're filmed by the media:

> "I keep thinking about all the kids who got wiped out by seventeen years of war movies before coming to Vietnam to get wiped out for good. You don't know what a media freak is until you've seen the way a few of those grunts would run around during a fight when they knew that there was a television crew nearby; they were actually making war movies in their heads, doing little guts-and-glory Leatherneck tap dances under fire, getting their pimples shot off for the networks. They were insane, but the war hadn't done that to them" (Herr 212).

3.   Conclusion

My thesis statement, that both writers depict the war without moral purposes, showing as well the negative features of the war (death, terror, fear, brutalization, deadening, etc.) as the properties of war which could be regarded as "positive" (a thrilling and seductive experience, comradeship, "beauty"/"majesty" of the war) has been confirmed. Neither of the both authors condemns or glorifies the war.Herr and O'Brien cover the Vietnam War in a subjective way, but in a frank and blunt fashion because they work out what the war meant to them. Tim O' Brien writes: "War is hell, but that's not the half of it, because war is also mystery and terror and adventure and courage and discovery and holiness and pity and despair and longing and love. War is nasty; war is fun. War is thrilling; war is drudgery. War makes you a man; war makes you dead" (O'Brien 77).

Dispatches and *The Things they carried* do not only confirm my thesis statement, they do it in a very similar way although they are made up from the two different literary categories Postmodernism and New Journalism. In fact, these categories are not so different because New Journalism originates in Postmodernism and it "blurs traditional genre distinctions in typical postmodern fashion" (Carpenter 36). The only real differences that I could make out in my comparision of *Dispatches* and *Things* are that O'Brien uses different narrative situations while Herr writes in a autobiographic manner and the fact that some aspects of O'Brien's 22 stories in Things are fiction, while Herr has produced a very subjective factual report in which the only fictional features are perhaps some exaggerated stories of American soldiers. The depiction of war is the same in both books, the authors share the same motives in which they describe Vietnam and they have the same opinion towards war, namely that one cannot say that war is good or bad.

Bibliography

Primary Sources

Herr, Michael. *Dispatches*. 1968. 48th ed. London: Picador, 2004.

O'Brien, Tim. *The Things They Carried*. London: Flamingo, 1991.

Secondary Sources

Carpenter, Lucas. "'It don't mean nothin': Vietnam War Fiction and Postmodernism." *College Literature* 30.2 (2003): 30-50.

Bonn, Maria S. "The Lust of the Eye: Michael Herr, Gloria Emerson and the Art of Observation." *Papers on Language and Literature: A Journal for Scholars and Critics of Language and Literature* 29.1 (1993): 28-48.

Hollowell, John. Fact and Fiction – The New Journalism and the Nonfiction Novel. The University of North Carolina, 1977.

Tegmark, Mats. *In the Shoes of a Soldier. Communication in Tim O'Brien's Vietnam Narratives*. Diss. Uppsala U, 1998. Acta Universitatis Upsaliensis. Studia Anglistica Upsaliensia 105. Uppsala, 1998.

Cuddon, John A. *A Dictionary of Literary Terms*. 4th ed. London: Penguin Books, 1999.

Murfin, Ross C., and Supryia M. Ray. *The Bedford glossary of critical and literary terms*. 2nd ed. Basingstoke: Palgrave, 2003.